Choose Confidence

21 Ways Women Can Increase Self-Confidence

Laura Diaz

Carmen,
wishing you the
best life to come.

Laura

www.inharmonycoaching.com

Cover design by Karen Floyd with Karen Floyd Photography
Editing by Andrea Susan Glass, www.WritersWay.com
Formatting by Trisha Fuentes

Disclaimer
The purpose of this book is to educate and empower. The author does not guarantee that anyone following these techniques, suggestions, tips, ideas, or strategies will achieve a particular result. However, if guidelines are followed, chances for success are increased. The author shall have neither liability nor responsibility with respect to any loss or damage caused, or alleged to be caused, directly or indirectly by the information contained in this book. Due to the evolving nature of the Internet, please note some resources may be out of date when you purchase this book. The resources cited are for the reader to research and are not necessarily endorsed by the author.

ISBN: 978-0-578-91426-8

Contents

Introduction

My story…

There I was… COMPLETELY terrified, my entire face bright red, my throat fully locked and my voice quivering, barely able to make a sound! I was paralyzed with fear.

No, this *wasn't* my reaction to coming face to face with a bear in the forest or finding myself confronted by a mugger. It was my body's reaction to being called on by my English teacher to stand and speak in front of the whole class!

You see, I grew up in a Mexican-American family where Spanish was my first language. Because of this I had a Mexican accent when speaking English and as a young child I was made fun of by my peers for the way I talked.

And as if it wasn't bad enough that I was so fearful of speaking, I actually believed that the kids in school, as early as elementary school, didn't like me BECAUSE I couldn't speak good English.

This led me to isolating myself—to hide so I wouldn't be teased or ridiculed by my classmates. This is when I first remember my low self-confidence showing up!

I was shy, introverted, wouldn't initiate conversations and kept to myself. Many emotions were running through me during those early years: unworthiness, shyness and anger. Because of these feelings I started to believe I wasn't "good enough"!

I know this is what led to my deep-seated embarrassment and tension whenever a teacher would call on me during class and ask me to speak. A sense of sheer terror would come over me! So, for the first 30 years of my life, I dreaded speaking in front of groups!

Even though I was scared of speaking in front of a classroom and groups, I knew deep down that I wanted something more in my life and this fear might hold me back. Later on, I realized that I had to, wanted to and believed I could get over this fear and allow that larger part of me to come out and express itself.

I didn't know what I had to do, so I decided to go on a journey to find ME. I engaged in personal development courses so I could explore my beliefs, habits, decisions and goals. What I discovered was that in order to create an extraordinary life, I had to have a strong belief that something inside me was superior and stronger than the outside circumstances. I knew I wanted to succeed in my career. I wanted upward career mobility and a good paying position. In order for me to reach that vision, I would have to increase my communication skills, interpersonal skills and self-esteem.

I realized I had a yearning for more success in my career and at the same time was aware that I needed to increase several work skills, mainly public speaking skills. Through my personal development studies, I learned that confidence empowers me to step out of my comfort zone. When you feel empowered and confident about how you approach life, you take control of your circumstances rather than allowing the circumstances to control you.

I remember clearly during my teenage years being fearful of rejection and as a consequence I wouldn't try anything new where I could fail. I believed I wasn't good enough. I was truly immobilized by fears and beliefs.

You may be wondering how you can be more confident and feel empowered. You may be struggling with your self-esteem and at times not feeling good enough. I've been there too. I'm sharing my personal experience in building self-confidence through the chapters in this book. I've learned different ways of being, thinking and relating that demonstrates confidence. I've taught classes on confidence. I've facilitated groups of women in building leadership skills, confidence and self-care. This is my first book and I wanted to dedicate it to describing 21 ways to build self-confidence.

Writing this book was a huge step in sharing what I know and have experienced in strengthening my confidence and helping other women build their confidence. Writing a book was not a priority in my life. However, in the fall of 2020, I attended a workshop given by my sales coach Eric Lofholm called "Write a Book in a Day." I found the title intriguing and since I'd been journaling for years, I decided to attend.

Eric discussed the topic of book titles and if we didn't have a title, he suggested we use "21 ways to _____." I decided to write a book about confidence since this has been the focus of my coaching business. I wrote down 21 ideas or ways how women can increase their confidence.

This book is for the woman who is looking for support in building her strength and feeling empowered. Through my professional experience I've met many women who were looking for support in building their confidence. There was a time I was one of those women and there were very few places I could find support.

I'm excited to share my journey with you as I approach writing this book with confidence. My hope is that you find the experiences, practices, tips and coaching suggestions as guidance for you to choose how you will develop your confidence.

#1 Self-Talk

Have you ever noticed how you talk to yourself? Have you ever noticed the ongoing chatter in your mind? Are your comments to yourself negative or positive?

I would guess that you have negative comments most of the time. I've learned that when you want to succeed at something or accomplish a goal, you must discipline your thoughts and the chatter. You have to pay attention to what you say to yourself.

At times you have feelings of anxiety and fear and may hold negative assumptions of what's going on presently or what the future holds. So as a consequence, you're talking to yourself based of these negative thoughts, assumptions and beliefs.

My suggestion is be intentional about shifting your thinking into positive and constructive thoughts. It would be helpful to develop an awareness of your toxic thoughts and perceptions. Notice what you're thinking and make a choice to not allow these thoughts to keep running. *How?*

By replacing negative thoughts with positive ones. This takes discipline and the more you engage with this practice, the easier it will be. Consciously choose to change your focus and step into the possibility of optimistic thoughts. Create a positive, self-empowering approach. Know that the only opportunity for change is in the present moment.

Through my studies in personal development and by working with teams, I learned that it's so important to speak positively and affirm my intentions as I engage in new ideas and practices in my work and personal life. I notice that when I speak in an optimistic manner to myself, I'm being optimistic. When I'm being confident with a task, I'm talking with courage, strength and confidence to myself as I engage in the task and I'm able to complete it easily.

Practice positive affirmations by making declarations of what you want and affirming that you're succeeding. One of my daily practices is to start the morning with quiet time, reading something inspirational and creating affirmations for the day. Two of my affirmations are "Today is going to be a good day" and "Good things are happening today."

I repeat these affirmations throughout the day to encourage my positive self-talk.

#2 Mindset

The definition of mindset is "a mental attitude or inclination" per Merriam-Webster's Collegiate Dictionary.

When you make up your mind to create positive changes in your life, and succeed, you start to create self-confidence. When I've studied the people, who've succeeded I found many of them had a plan for reaching their goals and each person devoted much thought and effort towards achieving that result.

Your confidence increases when you make an effort, believe in your abilities to achieve that goal and accomplish it. When you succeed with your goal, you increase your self-esteem and self-confidence. It feels good to work toward and reach a desired result and this is a great confidence booster.

My definition of being "confident" includes believing in yourself. When you believe you can attain a goal, your mind gets in motion to find a way. And you'll find many ways you can achieve what you want. Confidence is experienced when you take the first step towards the vision you have of your life.

Make a Decision to Succeed

Making a decision to succeed in life takes courage and following that mindset you need to take several steps. The first step is deciding you want to succeed at a goal. The second step is to commit to a plan of action. The third step would be to get started taking action. This path combines mindset, attitude and strategy!

My experience has been that you have to train your mind and attitude to be positive and think of success. Learning to be strategic is a mindset. If your mindset is to increase your confidence because you want to engage in a new career path, you intentionally have to create practices, new beliefs and associations that will support your mindset and results.

I've found that people who commit to their plan for personal development and are willing to do the work increase their chances of succeeding more than those who don't have a plan and don't take action. When you're focused with a plan, have a written strategy and take action, you create a momentum in your abilities and incrementally increase your enthusiasm and commitment towards succeeding at your goal.

Another technique of mindset I've discovered is to identify with success by creating affirmative declarations (affirmations) which I previously mentioned I do every day. "I am a successful business coach." "I am physically fit and healthy." "I am financially independent." Affirmations remind us to associate with that identity. Step into it with confidence that if it's not currently true, it will be soon.

These are a few examples of empowering positive statements. It helps for you to say them out loud daily until you're believing them and living them! So, no matter how you feel about your self-confidence right now, I believe you have it within you to be highly confident. This will take you on many successful paths.

I definitely know that your commitment to yourself is empowering. You'll act on what you want—if you want it enough—despite feelings of fear at times. You can't allow fear to hold you back. Consistent action will increase your self-confidence and reduce your fear and you'll discover more joy in your life. I know that it's worth it!

Your mindset is driving your conscious actions. Your mindset is foundational of who you are and how you show up in the world. The filters that make up our mindset come from our experiences, education and mental attitude of life. When you have a growth-oriented mindset to increase your work skills and qualities such as confidence, you'll make consistent efforts to increase your positive beliefs, habits and practices.

Mindset is so important in creating a life you want. If you want more confidence, you want to cultivate an attitude that you can do it and have the courage to go forward. Your confidence is demonstrated when you take the first step towards a goal you have set for yourself.

Mary, a coaching client, wanted to be assigned a special project within her work. She was shy and didn't feel confident in approaching her supervisor. We worked together for a few sessions in building her mindset. After some dialogue, we affirmed that Mary had the skills and experience to engage in this project.

We created a plan. I suggested some affirmative statements to say out loud to herself every day, such as "I'm the perfect person for this project" and "I'm so thankful for being assigned this project." She visualized receiving the assignment and got into the feelings of being excited and happy. After less than two weeks, she felt good enough about herself and with courage, she approached her supervisor and asked for the job. She was given the assignment of this special project. I was so happy for Mary in doing the work in building her mindset to take action and achieve the outcome she wanted.

#3 Your Vision

A vision is a dream you image for your future. Your imagination is the place where you start creating your future, where you image what you want in life and how you see yourself participating in your life.

Your vision is your destination. You start by deciding what future you want to live. What would you love to have in your life? The easiest way to create your vision is to think in categories and from there start making choices of what you would love to be, do and have.

What would you love with your health? What about your relationships with family, friends or co-workers? Look at your career and your work and consider what changes you would like to make. Let's not forget about your finances. Would you love to make more money and save more money? Would you love to invest? Your time is important so how would you love to spend your time?

When you have a vision of where you're going, a new level of confidence develops as you create goals and strategies and take action towards your vision. One of the first steps in moving toward riches, wealth and success is to have a clear, concise picture in your mind and in writing of what you're seeking. You want a vision that's so compelling that it pulls you forward with joy, anticipation and enthusiasm.

I've seen and experienced that without a clear destination in mind you're likely to continue to get the same results you've always had because you'll likely continue to revert to your past patterns. These old patterns haven't helped your confidence so it's time to cultivate new habits, beliefs and practices to ignite new confidence.

When I decided to create new ideas, practices and goals for myself, a new state of confidence was born that has taken me places in my career and personal life that I've always wanted to go.

The vision you create is your dream. I would encourage you to develop a relationship with your vision. Write it in a journal or someplace you'll see it often. When you strengthen your vision with daily contemplation, visualization and thought, you allow this vision to grow within you and ideas will come to fill in more details.

As you see this vison in your imagination, start having an attitude of expectation for it to come to you in its time or maybe sooner. When you take the first step into your dream, your vision, without knowing how it will happen, you're cultivating trust in yourself and in Universal Intelligence. You'll increase this faith through your imagination, will and focus and you'll start noticing positive results in your environment. This will allow you to feel a sense of confidence.

The unexpected could happen in that you may receive ideas on some strategies you can take toward areas of your vision. This has happened to me and it feels so magical!

This reminds me of what happened to Marilyn who had a goal to publish her aunt's book. She had a printed copy of her aunt's handwritten book. Marilyn decided to type up the book, edit it and get it ready for submission to a major publishing house. At the time, she didn't have a publisher in mind. She wanted to get it ready for publication, then get it published. So, she visualized the book being published.

Within a short time thereafter she received an invitation from Hay House which asked her if she was interested in getting the book published. She contacted them and was invited to talk with someone at Balboa Press, a part of Hay House. She submitted the manuscript, it was accepted and later published.

Decide to lead a vision-driven life. Realize that you're more powerful than your circumstances, situations and conditions. Live in a vision and refuse to live in circumstances!

Every year I create a vision for that year. I have a long-term vision for my life and career, health, family, relationships, money and time. All these cultivate my faith, belief in myself and my happiness. My vision directs my yearly goals. As I accomplish a higher number of my goals each year, my self-confidence increases.

As I work with my clients in life coaching, I encourage them to create a vision for their future living. This vision is a roadmap for them to create goals and build the life they desire.

#4 Goal Setting

Through my studies I learned of an explicit way to set goals. It's the SMART formula for setting goals. SMART is the acronym for Specific, Measurable, Attainable, Realistic and Timely.

Goals are meant for you to set your wants and wishes into action. Your goals gain momentum when they're something you *want* compared to something you *need*. There's no inspiration with needs; however, there is inspiration with wants. You need this inspirational fuel to keep you going towards accomplishment.

The truth is that only you can decide what goal is going to work best for you. When you commit to someone else's goal or you want to please another person, your chances of success are minimal!

At times your goal may be viewed as illogical. However, I discovered that not all goals are logical. Often when you have a wish, an idea or a dream and create a goal from there, you don't know 100% how to get it completed. Many goals you have are inspired and you'll have no idea how to achieve them. Yet, if you were inspired there is a way and it's only a matter of finding out how by trusting yourself. When you trust yourself, you become aware of abilities you didn't know you had.

When a goal is inspired, you'll tap into another source of energy and creativity. Some schools of thought call it Infinite Intelligence or Universal Intelligence. I believe there's an Infinite Intelligence into which we can all tap for ideas and resources.

Bob Proctor said this about goals: "The only prerequisite is, you must be able to see yourself on the screen of your mind, already in possession of the goal, and you must seriously want it." What I understand Mr. Proctor describing is you must see yourself in your imagination (your vision) as already in possession of your goal. Vision and goal-setting work together.

A worthwhile goal is one you don't know how to get—yet. However, if it's a goal you've imagined, you've created a vision in your mind and in writing and you see it as a possibility, it is worthwhile. The opportunity for you is finding out the "how."

You can find your how by being willing to search your inner resources, your outer resources and any ideas that come to you that give you a hint of how to find your how. When I've imagined a possibility and wrote about it in my journal, I've been inspired to create a vision, a possibility of my future. When I've done this and nurtured the vision, I noticed I was slowly creating a goal.

Once a goal is created in mind and in writing, ideas start coming through your mind, your heart and from other people. I've also discovered the how when I started taking the first step towards completing my goal. The beauty of this is that the completion of the first step leads to the second step and thereafter.

When I was willing to entertain a goal and see it in my mind, keeping it in my imagination, I was presented with ideas for manifestation. As long as I knew my "what," the "how" showed up later. It was source of magic at times; at least it felt that way to me.

Manifestation takes place rapidly when you write your goal, create steps to take and start taking action.

I find many people don't have a practice of setting goals or a plan to achieve their goals. Through my group coaching and classes, I've coached and taught many clients to set written goals, carve out time to take action towards the goal and have a deadline when the goal is expected to be completed. I hold them accountable for their progress and with support many achieve their goals.

Some comments I've received from group coaching and classes are "I liked the knowledge and the curriculum that was taught. It helped me to be less hard on myself." "I was excited to see how setting goals could be so simple. I wrote my goals and started to work towards my goals until I achieved them."

#5 Empowerment

Empowerment means to "enable or promote self-actualization" according to Merriam-Webster's Collegiate Dictionary.

We all have a storyteller in our mind. We're constantly having a dialogue with ourselves about what we want and at the same time telling ourselves the reasons we can't have what we want! Confidence is believing in your abilities to get results. You want to empower yourself to be a person of great esteem, skills, talents and confidence.

I want to share my experience of how I overcame my fear of speaking in front of groups and how overcoming this fear opened up new opportunities for me. I call this time the period when "I found my voice."

I Found My Voice

For a long time, I believed I couldn't speak in front of people. During high school and college, I didn't have the confidence or courage to speak in class. I had been hesitating for the first 30 years of my life to speak in front of groups! I remember the embarrassing and tense moments I experienced when the teacher would call on me during class and I was asked to stand and speak. I would feel afraid and nervous as I started to speak.

Now I can speak with ease and confidence in front of groups. I enjoy being a teacher, speaker and life coach and leading classes and groups. I feel good about who I am and what I'm expressing through my words. My beliefs have changed significantly through the choice I made of asking for help with training and practice in being a professional speaker and teacher. My activities now include speaking often with small groups and classes.

I made the choice one day that I wanted upward mobility and didn't want to be passed over for promotion. I was ready to empower myself and deal with my fear of speaking in front of people. This fear was holding me back from being promoted and from asking for help with my career.

I wanted to succeed in my career and I wanted more administrative/managerial positions. When I realized it was important that I speak confidently in front of groups, I did my research and joined a Toastmistress group. Now, I experience less anxiety and self-consciousness. I experience more freedom, flexibility and self-confidence.

If someone is struggling with similar challenges, I would advise them to join a speaking group and engage in the practice of speaking. It's difficult to overcome this fear without help and having the support and training of a professional group accelerates your personal growth in speaking and building confidence.

A core belief shift I support is that we all have a message and if you find a way to speak and share your gifts and talents, you'll make a significant contribution to others as well as yourself in many ways.

I can tell you now that it was worth the time, training and practice. My transformation into being at ease with my newfound self-confidence was wonderful! I transformed myself into being less anxious and more social and I learned how to make small talk with strangers. Shy me, who was too shy to be noticed and speak up, now was not afraid to start a conversation with a stranger.

I would suggest you take an inventory of what skills you need to learn so you're more self-actualized and can play a bigger game in life. When you empower yourself to increase a life skill, you empower your confidence.

What choices do you want to make for your career and personal development? What skills do you want to strengthen? What qualities do you want to build in your character? Who do you want to be in the next 10 years? Answering these questions will give you some insight into what areas you need to empower.

#6 Education

The dictionary definition of education is "the act or process of teaching or being taught."

As you engage in schooling, college, professional training and work experience you acquire education in your career and in the role you play. You develop your skills, expertise and confidence by engaging in the study of a work skill and practicing these skills on the job.

A misconception I've heard is that some people think you automatically grow mentally, spiritually and emotionally because you're growing and aging chronologically. This is not so.

As you age, if you don't educate yourself about life, career and how to overcome daily challenges, you'll have difficulty dealing with various life situations.

I've found that it takes a willingness to learn about life and yourself in order to succeed. Self-confidence comes from your willingness to engage with your life. There's so much to learn about life, work, relationships, money and personal freedoms, that you'll always be learning something new every day of your life.

What's amazing is that you have an intelligence that wants to continue learning and becoming. You're constantly in the moment of change. Making a decision to do something different is a decision to be in the process of transformation.

When you want success in your career, your life and your health, you need to set goals and internal intentions of who you want to become. Becoming is a process you have to create willingly with some discipline and re-training of your thinking and actions. Education is so important for your personal development!

When I decided in my mid-30s that I wanted to overcome the fear of speaking in groups and in front of people, this was a learning process for me. I was willing to learn by joining Toastmistress, attending meetings and practicing giving talks. This wasn't always easy.

The reason this was so important to me was that I wanted to be promoted in my career and I wanted to overcome my fear of speaking in front of groups. This fear was holding me back in my career and personal relationships. Once I made a decision to learn public speaking, this decision opened the way to new positive ideas and enriching relationships.

What is it that you want in life? Are you willing to learn new ideas and new ways of thinking as well as new ways of being? If so, you're on the road to increasing your confidence!

Confidence is trusting in yourself to push past your fears and not giving up because of fear! Acting in spite of fear adds to your courage, confidence and belief in yourself.

Confidence is something you give yourself. Some ways to build your self-confidence are:

- *Learn more about yourself.* Explore topics, subjects that interest you and study new ideas. I enjoy reading and sharing ideas. A few years from the time I started my coaching business, I discovered I enjoyed teaching as I was sharing ideas with a small group. As a consequence, I decided to teach classes with a local organization and through my coaching practice.

- *Become more effective in one area of your life.* If one area interests you in your career, find a way to up-level your skills. One that I've become more effective in is using Microsoft PowerPoint for my classes.

- *Like yourself better.* When you like yourself better, you'll treat yourself with kindness. A practice I've used is to write a list of what good things are in my life. I read this list often and feel grateful. When you're feeling good and grateful, you feel powerful. When you feel powerful, you're more confident.

- *Focus on positive mindset.* If you want success in your career and life, take ownership of creating a positive mental attitude. Whatever you focus on expands. When I decided to open my coaching business, I had a strong conviction and belief in myself that I could succeed. From that belief I created programs, classes and presentations. Within a few years, I succeeded in building a coaching business with a small team.

- Trust that you know what works best for you. As you gain experience, have ups and downs and learn lessons, you develop a trust in what works for you. This is your life and you have to engage and be willing to risk failing to realize what will work for you.

#7 Self-Esteem

S elf-esteem—or how you see and think of yourself—is essential in building self-confidence. I learned to build my self-esteem by consciously showing appreciation for myself. This isn't something I was taught to do growing up.

Often as children we're discouraged from speaking positively about ourselves and shamed if we do by being judged as acting conceited or showing off. The consequence of this is that we remain quiet when we want to share positive thoughts about ourselves for fear of being labeled as bragging.

What happens if we hide ourselves? We learn to play small and be small. So as adults it's important to take time with ourselves and show appreciation. How?

I suggest you create a list of what you appreciate about yourself. Maybe write a list every week or even daily of what you like about yourself. Do this exercise on a consistent basis.

I notice that as I appreciate myself, I'm more accepting of myself. Self-acceptance is part of self-esteem because it's about accepting all parts of who we are, the perfect and imperfect self. We're human beings in the process of becoming the best we can at any moment.

These are some strategies I use for myself and with my coaching clients:

- Create goals in any three areas of your life such as career, family, health, money or relationships.

- Work towards your goals in small steps.

- Learn something new that helps you accomplish your goals with ease and grace.

- Reach out for mentors or coaches who can help you expand and navigate your challenges.

- Create a spiritual ritual to inspire you to continue on your quest to expand.

After an intensive workshop, one of my clients stated, "I began to feel better. As I worked on the exercises, received coaching and began challenging myself to look deep I shifted my perspective and gained the knowledge to make some positive changes."

#8 Agreements

Keeping our agreements with ourselves can be a challenge. After studying the book, *The Four Agreements* by Don Miguel Ruiz, I started to appreciate the value of keeping my agreements. One of the agreements in his book is to "be impeccable with your word."

I found it was essential to cultivate trust with myself as I was on the path of personal transformation and becoming a leader in my career. When I started keeping agreements with myself, I increased my trust and I also noticed that my self-esteem and self-confidence increased.

I find it's common to hear that people promise themselves they'll do something and later they don't keep their agreement. They make an excuse or make up a good reason why they didn't follow through.

We think this is okay because no one knows we messed up or we think we can do it later. However, later may not come and the promise we made with ourselves can be shelved to "someday."

Remember, any kind of agreement you make with yourself is as important as any agreement you make with another person. For example, when you say, "I'll take a walk tomorrow morning" and then you don't because you didn't feel like it, this is an excuse and a breach of your agreement.

After my experiences of keeping and not keeping my agreements, I realized it made a difference in how I saw myself. As a result of keeping my agreements, I increased the trust with myself, I built a confidence in my decisions and I increased my self-esteem.

Now I deliberately make agreements only if I intend to keep them. If I don't for some good reason, I re-negotiate my agreement. Do I always keep my agreements with myself? Not 100%! Like most people, I'm a work in progress and I'm working purposely to keep my agreements more often than not.

#9 Optimism

Expect good things to happen to you and expect the best is coming. This is an optimistic attitude you can adopt.

I'm very grateful for discovering the topic of optimism. I've studied several masters on this topic and have integrated some beliefs of optimism that work for me.

When I adopted the principles of optimism, I opened the way to a positive outlook on life. Since then, I've been more willing to tackle new ventures instead of doubting myself and being afraid to try something new because I expect to fail or be rejected.

A practice that has really helped me to be optimistic is being vigilant with the thoughts that come through my mind. I've learned that thoughts that come through me may not always be the truth.

A focus I practice daily is to have a positive outlook on the day. When I take that perspective, I can decide what thoughts to agree with and adopt them as true for me. For example, when I take on the perspective "that today is going to be a good day," my intention is to notice what is good about the day. Of course, during the day something may happen that isn't good and when that happens, I notice that I don't get as emotionally upset as I used to when I didn't have this optimistic mindset.

I know I have random thoughts which repeatedly go through my mind and I do my best to choose only the positive thoughts that bring hope, faith and love to my consciousness.

You may have heard the idea that you are what you believe. So, if you want to have a positive perspective and believe in good outcomes, you have to make the effort and consciously choose your thoughts.

Our thoughts and words have power. Every word and every thought have energy and they affect our mood and attitude, so when we consciously choose optimistic viewpoints and attitudes, we're also cultivating an inner confidence.

I'm grateful I've discovered my inner strengths of faith and positivity. I feel a strong sense of confidence in who I am becoming as a woman and as a professional.

#10 Beliefs

Through our upbringing, family, school and culture, we adopted our beliefs of what we think is right and wrong.

Beliefs are what we've decided in our mind and way of living to be true. This is an area that as adults we may question. Often, we realize that what we believed or had a strong conviction about wasn't true and hasn't worked for our benefit.

When I started my journey in personal development, I became more aware of my beliefs and how they influenced my choices. I wasn't always happy with the choices I made. Through the help of my mentors, I learned to question and explore my beliefs and in time decided to change the beliefs that weren't working for my good.

One area I work with my clients on through my life coaching is the exploration of beliefs and habits. I suggest you start noticing your beliefs and which ones have helped you achieve success and which beliefs hold you back.

As I've said one of my core beliefs when I was younger was that I didn't speak in front of groups because I believed I didn't communicate well. Later on, through my self-development, I realized that this belief wasn't helping me move forward in my career and it wasn't improving my self-esteem. If I had kept that belief and done nothing about it, I would have remained in the same place.

Once I was trained with skills for public speaking, my other challenge was applying for a management position. Part of me believed I could do the job with training and there was another part of me that was scared and doubtful about being in a position of management.

Prior to applying for a promotion as team manager, I had participated in several personal development courses and had been participating for one year with my speaking group. So with this training, I developed stronger confidence and a belief that I could do the job as a team manager.

What helped me most in staying with my speaking group was the support of the members in moving through my fear, doubt and nervousness. My belief in what I could do professionally increased with the support of my speaking group and mentors within this group.

The following are beliefs I've cultivated that have helped me succeed:

- I believe I'm intelligent.

- I believe I'm doing something good for myself and others.

- I believe I'm here to serve others through my coaching and mentoring.

- I believe I have the resources to accomplish my goals.

- I believe that the Universe/God is supporting me in doing good deeds.

I realized that beliefs are your opinion of what you describe as your reality. Your beliefs contribute to building your life and who you become. Your beliefs add to your self-confidence or take away from it.

I suggest you make a list of what positive beliefs you have about yourself. A list of your attributes can be motivating in persisting through difficult moments and will definitely boost your confidence.

#11 Self-Leadership

In any given moment you can choose to be a victim of the circumstance or be a self-leader. As a self-leader you take responsibility for your choices and decisions.

Life happens and you're constantly having to choose consciously or react unconsciously as to how to respond. If you look back on how you were brought up, what beliefs you adopted, what behaviors you considered normal and what responses were expected, you can get a picture of whether you're reacting to your circumstances or coming from a position of leadership.

"Self-leaders know the significance and impact of being resourceful over having resources," says Jason Goldberg author of *Prison Break*. In his book Jason writes about how self-leaders own their interpretations and respond to circumstances, while prisoners of circumstance feel helpless, powerless of the circumstances and are most likely bystanders waiting for the circumstances to dictate their next action or choice. Self-leaders see situations as conditions of the game of life and initiate an action from their own interpretations.

Think about how you make decisions. Are you making them based on your conditions or do you examine your resources, both tangible and intangible, when making a decision?

Do you make decisions because something "should be a certain way?" Or do you pause and review your options? You can do this by reflecting on what you want and making a responsible choice instead of relying on what the circumstances suggest.

During numerous courses and training, I learned that I make decisions through many filters. These are programs I was conditioned to accept and from there I make my decisions.

As I increased my self-leadership skills, I realized that some of my filters don't support me as a woman or for someone who wants to be in a position of leadership. I slowly found ways to re-pattern some beliefs, habits and filters I was using in making decisions.

I found that my confidence grew as I took courageous actions that had me examining my filters, beliefs and behaviors that didn't support my future success.

You have the ultimate responsibility in defining who you are and how you'll design your life. You decide how you'll respond to life, moment by moment.

As a self-leader, what are you willing to be in creating a happy and successful life? One of my beliefs is that I, you and everyone deserve to live with joy, happiness and abundance. And because of this belief, I have engaged in continual professional learning, empowering my leadership skills as well as my life and business coaching skills.

I believe in the work I do as a life and business coach. I love working with people and helping them navigate through their challenges and beliefs. I've seen through numerous people

I have coached an amazing transformation when they challenge their beliefs that are holding them from their dreams.

Self-leadership is about taking responsibility for your life and making choices that add to your happiness and joy.

#12 Choices

By the time I was in my late 30s I knew something had to change. I was tired of watching other people advance in their careers while I continued to let fear hold me back.

I had to make a choice: either give up on my managerial aspirations or do something about my fear of public speaking! Do I stay safe and give up or do I do something about my fear?

I was at a crossroad and I had to make a choice.

Have you ever been in a situation in which you had to make a difficult choice? A choice between a better future or a safe present? A choice to either face a BIG FEAR or compromise on your goals? If so, then you KNOW it's NOT easy.

I knew my situation couldn't stay the same, so I decided to trust that inner part that said "go!" I still remember my first speaking training meeting. Everyone at the meeting seemed so confident and comfortable speaking and they were much more advanced than I expected them to be. I was SO intimated that besides introducing myself I barely said a word.

But I kept going. I knew I had to. And looking back, I can tell you now that despite the fear and discomfort I felt during those first few meetings it was worth the time, training and practice that I put into continuing to attend.

And I DO mean practice! Even though I felt embarrassed, nervous and insecure, I committed to consistently doing the speech exercises at each meeting. Close to one year of increasing my speaking skills, I started to feel confident in my abilities and had more trust in what I was doing. Not only did my public speaking abilities improve but I noticed several other changes due to my newfound confidence. I was engaging more with people and making small talk with strangers. My self-confidence was lifted due to overcoming a BIG fear and accomplishing a BIG goal!

Did I have moments when I felt afraid, anxious, doubtful and embarrassed? Of course! But I was committed to making this work for me! I could never imagine that overcoming this challenge could open so many new doors in my life and career.

Now, years later, I enjoy being a teacher, speaker and life and business coach and I often lead classes and groups. I no longer feel embarrassed or self-conscious and my words flow effortlessly.

When I made a choice for a bigger version of me and faced my challenge, fears and uncertainty, I welcomed the leader in me to step up. I learned how to run meetings, how to take on leadership positions within the club, how to organize a presentation, how to interview and how to make small talk with a stranger. All these skills were transferrable skills that later assisted me in my future managerial position.

Now I experience less anxiety and self-consciousness of how I look and how I speak. And I experience more freedom, flexibility and confidence.

The learned skill of public speaking opened many doors to me in occupations, promotions and new training opportunities.

If I had not taken this massive step towards overcoming my greatest fear, I'm not sure I would have been as successful as I have been in my career!

Because of this it's now my mission to support ambitious women struggling with low self-confidence to overcome their fears of being seen and heard so they can work towards thriving in their life and career.

We ALL have some degree of confidence which can be built up by being true to ourselves and overcoming challenges that hold us back from succeeding. Being confident was a choice I made during one of my crossroad moments. I'm grateful for this choice since the leader in me emerged and now I create coaching programs to help other women break through their low confidence.

What really can help you make a choice during your crossroad moments is having a strong vision and goals of where you want to go in your life and profession.

Sara made a choice to receive coaching. She wanted to create structure and to be held accountable for her goals. She told me, "Coaching services have inspired me to set and achieve goals." With ongoing coaching and structure, Sara accomplished several projects. During coaching she learned the value of making and keeping a commitment. Her choice to continue with coaching has helped her create a structure, accountability and commitment to her results.

#13 Self-Care

Taking care of yourself and your well-being is so important in living a healthy and prosperous life! What does self-care mean to me? Self-care means:

- Liking who I am

- Enjoying my own company

- Feeling at peace with myself

- Being creative with my ideas

- Feeling joyful and having experiences that add to my joy

- Taking care of my basic physical, emotional, spiritual and mental needs

When I view self-care as a practice of self-love, this increases my self-confidence. I feel confident that I have my primary needs handled and from there I can take on the world. What that also means is that I engage in certain activities that support my self-care.

Some of my daily practices include creating a morning ritual. I wake up early, make coffee to enjoy the morning and read positive affirmations to welcome the day. I write a list of gratitude in my journal. As I write my gratitude's for the day, I'm filled with joy and peace.

I read inspirational books that feed my mind and emotions. I reflect about what I write, what I read and then journal my thoughts. Sometimes as I'm journaling, ideas for new coaching programs come up.

My morning ritual time is about two hours and it's a grounding time for me to start the day. This morning ritual acknowledges me as a worthy person, provides love and affirms my existence. It's essential for my self-care.

Self-care is more than saying you're taking care of yourself. It's making time for your self-care. It's honoring the time you schedule for your self-care and avoiding distractions that will disrupt your self-care. This is the time that making an appointment with yourself is so important to keep and honor.

We're living in a fast-paced society. We have the Internet, television 24 hours and technology rapidly making changes in how we live. All this can create stress, overwhelm and health challenges.

This reminds me of Betty who was working 40+ hours a week, going to evening school to complete her Master's degree and making time for her family. As a consequence, she was feeling out of balance, stressed and grouchy. When we started working together, we agreed on a self-care program. I recommended she start a morning ritual of waking up earlier so she had enough time to feel relaxed, quiet her mind with a short meditation, read some inspiration material and journal her thoughts. I ask that she start with 30 minutes each morning during her working week.

After a few weeks of trying to keep a consistent schedule engaging in this morning ritual, she was able to commit to 30 minutes Monday through Friday. After a month, she noticed her stress levels were reduced, she felt more at peace and didn't feel so rushed. She was able to make more effective decisions at work and her relationships at work and at home improved.

Self-care is an important habit that helps sustain a healthy and productive life. Having self-care tools, routines and practices feeds your self-esteem and well-being.

#14 Intuition

Intuition is defined as "the immediate knowing or learning of something without conscious use of reasoning; instantaneous apprehension." I take this to mean that our intuition is our inner knowing. I've experienced intuition as an immediate knowing or nudging and I've also experienced it as ideas coming into my thought process unexpectedly.

When I've experienced intuitive nudges and flashes of insight, I feel inspired, lifted and motivated to take action. I claim these nudges and insights as my "still small voice" talking with me. I claim my intuition has a big part of my inner confidence, that part inside that knows what is right for me. It's that part that feels good and I could easily say it's another definition of intuition.

Through my studies in personal development and spirituality I've learned that intuition is a mental faculty that isn't concerned with reason. It points the way, leaving you free to take it or leave it.

During my earlier years my beliefs about intuition were minimal and I didn't give my intuitive feelings importance when making a choice. Today my intuition is of great importance when making a choice! When I have a choice to make, I spend some quiet time reflecting on what my intuition is leaning towards. I've made major decisions with my intuition nudging me to go a certain way such as when I decided to retire from my job as a Team Manager.

During my late 50s I was working as a Team Manager and I enjoyed the work. However, I started to feel a nudge that was suggesting it was time for me to make a career change because there was something that was incomplete! What? I didn't know!

So, two years before I decided to retire from state service, I hired a life coach to help me explore this nudging. During my coaching I decided I wanted to look into training as a life coach. When I explored the coach training programs at Accomplishment Coaching, I experienced a strong intuitive feeling that said, "You are home! This is it!"

I enrolled in the coaching program for one year. Becoming a life coach was a natural transition on my personal journey into my new period that was called "retirement". As I experienced an emotional embrace, I decided at that moment that life coaching was my next career!

I had to re-assess my life purpose. The transition to life coaching has been fun and empowering and has lifted my self-confidence in many ways. Being a life coach has been transformational and I have re-invented who I am. I've experienced less confusion, anxiety and uncertainty of what's next in my life—creating who I am as a life coach and contributing to other people through my coaching and training programs.

It's important that we learn more about our inner guidance system because our soul speaks through our intuition.

#15 Facing Challenges

Every day you face challenges. In facing challenges, you learn about yourself and how you interact with other people and situations. In facing challenges, you may not know what to do and what's the right approach to take in solving a problem or task.

Since you're constantly learning, facing an uncertain time or task is very common. This is the time to either ask for help or go inward to find an answer. You'll find that you have a wealth of information stored within that can come to the rescue. One way to bring up solutions is to ask yourself questions.

For example, let's say you want to create financial independence. One question you can ask is, "What's the first step I can take with what I have to create financial independence?" As you contemplate this question and remain silent, you'll notice ideas coming up of what first step you can take.

A mindset that helps in facing challenges is creating a positive outlook for your life. What that means to me is live with optimism and expect the best. That takes some study and practice. I recommend reading and studying laws of success and optimism.

Go beyond what you think you can do! I've learned that when you stretch yourself in moving forward towards an awesome goal, you'll receive inner direction and confidence and your mindset will kick in to assist you in making results happen.

When you carry a positive attitude of who you are and what good you're contributing to your community, unexpected support comes to assist you. Believe that anything is attainable. The bigger the challenge, the more you rise to the occasion and you play a bigger game. When you make a decision to play a bigger game, you engage in learning more about yourself, work skills, habits and beliefs. By this I mean you start engaging in accomplishing your dreams, goals and desires and from there your personal transformation occurs.

Certain circumstances demand that you step up to a bigger challenge at times. Don't back out! Step into the challenge and see a bigger you evolve into playing a bigger game. You may never know your untapped potential unless you tap it when taking on a bigger challenge. Who knows what could be beneath the surface? Unless you think big enough you might not know or realize how extraordinary you are!

One of my ongoing challenges is building and up-leveling my coaching business. What has worked for me in developing my coaching business has been to build a team of other professionals who can support me with my business. Other professionals I've hired are mentor-coaches, a virtual assistant, a copywriter and a bookkeeper.

Facing challenges is easier when you cultivate a positive mindset on life, reach out for assistance and trust yourself that you can accomplish your goals.

Between 2015 and 2019, I volunteered at a residential recovery program to conduct group coaching and life skills. The monthly group coaching provided support for the women in the program who were facing challenges and helped to develop life and career skills. We covered topics like mindset, gratitude, self-esteem and career skills to name a few. I often heard from the women who said they gained a deeper understanding of their strengths, determination and passion to make empowering choices that prompted their health, passions, self-esteem and career options. The group sessions provided guidance in creating short-term and long-term goals.

#16 Dreams

Dreams are our imagination, desires, hopes, wishes and goals that we want for our future. Defining dreams is not easy because you could define them as something you think about often. You could say that dreams are made up fantasies.

Dreams are your aspirations and hopes of what you would love in the future. I feel dreams are our inspiration for designing a future that brings happiness and joy. When we're in a state of happiness and joy, we take on a state of confidence.

I believe we can make our dreams come true. I've experienced many times my dreams coming into reality. Some of my dreams that came true were:

- Finishing college with a Master's degree

- Completing a law degree

- Overcoming the fear of public speaking

- Buying my first house before the age of 30

The beauty of having dreams is that you can select which dreams you want to shape your future. Dreams are close to our soul's purpose in finding joy and happiness. When you're coming from a dream you've imaged and then find a way to bring it into reality, you're living in harmony with your soul's purpose. Your imagination can help you build your dream and find ways to bring it into reality.

I attended Mary Morrissey's DreamBuilder™ Live seminar. This was the first time that I learned to live from my vision, not my circumstances. That was a huge game changer for me. As I reflected on my life, I realized that I'd been making plans and setting goals based on my surrounding conditions. For example, if I didn't have the money to invest in vocational or personal development training, that I wanted to better my future, I wouldn't spend the money.

After the training in dream building, I found a way to declare my dream, create a clear blueprint for my dreams and make a commitment to build my dreams.

The challenge is your willingness to get bigger than your conditions (i.e., not enough money). When you're going for a dream that's important to you, you'll find resources and opportunities that will support you in helping you achieve your dreams.

One year prior to my retirement, I visited Accomplishment Coaching Programs during a morning of observation of the coaching trainees. I had been working with my life coach in deciding my next career, which was life coaching. I was planning on submitting my retirement papers and was looking to re-invent my future with another career.

After being inspired by the coach training and making a decision to attend the following year, the next challenge was finding the money. Intuitively I felt that this was the next training I wanted to engage in. Since I had a strong desire to be in this coach training program, with the help from my life coach we found a way for me to finance the program.

I created a plan for my dream of being a trained life coach, as well as becoming a certified DreamBuilder™ coach. I engaged with Mary Morrissey's DreamBuilder™ Coaching Program and received my certification to teach others about the DreamBuilding program. Dream building starts with your thinking. You start by asking yourself, "What would I love in this area of my life?" This question unlocks your imagination with ideas to start creating your dreams.

Successful people begin with the end in mind, that is, they know their outcome. They become clear on what they really want. They focus on their dreams, then create a vision from these dreams and then set goals.

I leave you with a question: What would you love in your future? I invite you to journal on this question and listen to your intuition for answers.

#17 Expertise and Experience

What are you an expert in? For one thing I know that you're an expert on your life. The experiences, skills and education you have contribute to your confidence and how you show up in this world.

Feel credible and confident from within! As we review some factors, you'll find evidence to back up your credibility and confidence. Credibility comes from the inside. It's a quality of being trusted, believed in. It's also a quality in which you believe in yourself and you trust yourself that you can make a difference. You can make a difference!

Life gives you moments to show your expertise, skills, experience and competencies in life, in work and in being who you are. I believe you are constantly given the opportunity to reinvent who you are.

Your credibility has been rewarded by the awards, promotions, testimonials and acknowledgements you've received. Take a moment and write a list of awards, leadership roles you've taken, skills you've learned, strengths you've developed and vocational achievements you've had. All of these and more show your expertise and experience. This adds to your self-confidence.

I'm inviting you to do this now. When you notice your accomplishments, you'll feel a warm feeling of strength within which is your confidence coming through. Keep this list and add to it to acknowledge how much you've accomplished and feel proud of your experiences and expertise.

As you strive to be a better version of yourself each year, you're continuously reinventing and up-leveling your mindset to pull you forward with new changes. What new skills and knowledge are you learning? How are you up-leveling yourself?

As you feed your mind with positive empowering material and hold a belief for something bigger in your life, you're simultaneously taking action to be in alignment with your mindset.

Think of your credibility as your bank account. Think of your credibility as a tool to build your self-confidence. With your experience, skills and credibility you build an identity from which you see yourself. You want to build an image of yourself as a confident person.

#18 Courage

What does it mean to have courage and to use courage as you face new challenges? The definition of courage is "mental or moral strength to venture, preserve and withstand danger, fear or difficulty."

How many times have you had to face fear, difficulty and maybe danger and you found your inner strength and mental ability to go forward despite the fear, difficulty and danger? I believe we're born with courage and it's a muscle we build with time through facing difficult circumstances.

You use courage when you have a vision or a goal. When you have the ambition to make a positive change in your life, you'll be using courage to go beyond your fear and discomfort.

One example of where I used courage to accomplish a goal was when I attended a Warrior Camp several years ago in the early 2000s. One of the challenges was walking over hot coals. When I was first told that I had a choice to walk the hot coals, my initial reaction was "No, I'm scared and I'm going to get burnt!"

As I walked with the group to the outside land where the fire department was monitoring the hot coals, I told myself that I wasn't going to participate. I kept repeatedly telling myself "I'm not going to walk the coals." As I stood with others in the group, I felt anxious, scared and vigilant of my surroundings.

After a few minutes, I noticed people running through the hot coals with ease. Even though I was scared, something inside of me said "You can do it." So, I changed my mind and decided to walk the coals.

I stood in line and as I approached the front of the walk, two counselors coached me to focus on a positive goal as I ran through the hot coals. I was coached for a few minutes until I had a positive mindset and goal to carry me through.

Once I decided on my goal and truly believed in my ability to walk without injury, I focused on the other side of the coals where another counselor was waiting for my arrival. I kept thinking only of my goal. My eyes were on my destination, the counselor. I didn't look down at the coals. I ran as fast as I could. I made it through in less than a few seconds and I didn't burn my feet. I was elated as I embraced the counselor on the other side of the coals! I did it!

This experience has carried me in moments when I've had to rely on my courage. What I proved to myself is that I can do what I place in my mind to do and take action upon.

I've faced many challenges in my work and personal life and courage has played a big part in my facing fear with courage. This mental and moral strength has been a strong foundation in building my future with confidence.

And I feel happy, very happy, about these courageous decisions which have helped me to become a better version of myself. Step out in courage and go for all you desire in work and life.

#19 Personal Development

Brain Tracy said, "Personal development is a major time-saver. The better you become, the less time it takes you to achieve your goals."

Personal development is a process in which you learn skills, qualities and set goals to maximize your potential. It's about developing skills that will improve you personally and professionally.

After college when I joined the workforce as a full-time professional counselor in the mid-1970s is when I started to experience what it meant to be in a place of personal power. In my early working years, I experienced the difference of how women and men were treated in the workforce. I noticed men were more frequently seen as leaders.

During this time, I was in a place of seeing myself as a good worker, wanting promotions and at the same time nourishing peer/work relationships. I started to notice the low confidence of the women in moving towards advancements and promotions. I also noticed my own low self-confidence in not believing I could one day go into management.

I believed that what held me together and kept me believing I could someday be a manager were the personal development classes I was taking on my own time. The classes, studies and mentors helped me believe I could advance in my career. I identified several skills I needed to learn before I could apply for a promotion.

My entry into the workforce was a time of huge transformation for me and it was the quick start that moved me rapidly towards increasing my personal leadership skills and self-confidence.

I'm giving you the history of my work and personal experience to show you some background of how I went through a period of conquering my fears and periods of low self-confidence and the professional initiative I took to move from that place of not feeling or acting like the leader I wanted to be to learning to be a more effective leader in my life and career.

One of the strategies for building your self-confidence is learning more about you. I found great value in studying Napoleon Hill's *Keys to Success*. In this book I learned about taking personal initiative when building your success and leadership skills. One of the strategies of personal development is taking initiative in realizing your goals.

Some of the attributes of personal initiative are the qualities of:

- Self-reliance

- Self-discipline

- Persistence

- The habit of going the extra mile

- Assuming full responsibility for one's own actions

The qualities of personal initiative are important in building confidence, strength and resilience in yourself. These qualities are important in building your personal development of goals, skills and strategies for success. As a woman who wanted to be successful in her career it was essential that I studied the laws of success and worked on strategies that would build me beyond who I was.

As you learn more about yourself you realize what you need to learn, what you need to change and what's important to you and your future. When you know you're on the path of the life you want, you're more willing to take personal initiative in creating a plan, goals, structure and support system.

One way to start is to decide where you're going in your life and career. Then look at where you are and what you have to do to get started on your path. Also review your habits and beliefs that may not support you and the habits and beliefs that will support you. What changes do you need to make so you can build a strong foundation of beliefs, habits and practices to succeed?

Confidence is standing strong as a leader. I made a choice to increase my skills in management, communication and interpersonal skills. These skills increased my leadership and confidence in moving forward in my career.

Personal development is an ongoing process. There will always be something new to learn in your life and in your career.

#20 Gratitude

There's been a lot written about gratitude. I've come to the conclusion that gratitude is essential for our happiness, well-being and prosperity!

Gratitude is the expression of appreciation. Research studies of the brain and people expressing gratitude have revealed that those who express gratitude feel happier, more alive and healthier.

When you're in a place of happiness and well-being, you're in a place of self-confidence. Gratitude is important because it helps you feel good and it inspires you to do good. Gratitude heals, energizes, inspires and transforms your life in many ways.

I have a gratitude practice. I've noticed that I feel good about myself as I write my gratitude statements. Feeling good is about cultivating my self-esteem. Feeling good is also about being confident.

I journal every morning and make a list of what I'm grateful for. Some of my statements are, "I'm happy and grateful that I'm healthy; I'm grateful for today because it's going to be a good day." I feel it's important to have gratitude for what we have as well as what we've achieved.

This powerful exercise encourages me to be reflective and appreciative of what I have in my life. I know that the more I recognize what I have, how I use it and how I share what I have with others, the more is given to me in various forms. Gratitude is being conscious of your existence and creating a practice of acknowledgment which is life-giving.

Gratitude builds a spiritual muscle that enhances your self-esteem and confidence. Several research studies with diverse groups have revealed that the practice of gratitude leads to the following:

- Increased good feelings of energy and enthusiasm
- Enhanced feelings of happiness and joy
- Improved feelings of self-worth and self-confidence

I would suggest you add a gratitude practice to your daily self-care. Start by writing three items you're grateful for each day. Adding gratitude to your day gives you an experience of feeling good. When you feel good, this adds to your self-esteem and confidence.

#21 Demonstrate Confidence

True confidence isn't created because of what you do. It's created by your belief in the ability you have to do anything you want to do. The dictionary defines confidence as "the quality or state of certain."

Throughout this book I've described different topics, strategies and experiences of how to build your self-confidence. There's so much more to say on this topic but for now I'll end this book with an overall discussion of the topic of confidence.

Creating a life, you love and achieving the results you want starts with a deeper understanding about yourself. Learning about yourself is about exploring your beliefs, habits, goals and resources to see if they're in support of reaching your goals and achieving success.

Confidence is a quality, a strength you demonstrate in your thoughts, behavior, mindset and way of being. When you take on new challenges in life, this is the time you may question the level of confidence you have. You question if you have the strength to go forward. You may question if you have the education and knowledge to figure it out and to know what steps to take. Overall, you examine what you know to determine if you have the inner strength and fortitude to take courageous action.

Developing self-confidence is about making a choice to develop your strength, character, and mindset in moving forward with courage and insight. When I coach someone in developing their self-confidence, we start by examining where they are now. We take an inventory of their strengths, blessings, talents and resources. Next, we review their beliefs and habits and evaluate which ones will help them increase their self-confidence and reach their goals.

Increasing self-confidence does take work. It takes looking at your life and examining the beliefs you hold that have you living the way you're currently living. It takes looking at how you see yourself, how you identify as a human being. It takes identifying what you think is missing in your life and what needs to happen for you to attain what's missing.

During my life coaching I work with clients on interrupting thinking and beliefs. When you realize that how you see yourself and the world affects the results you get, then we can start making a plan of what changes need to happen for you to develop your confidence.

Most of us would like to have more confidence. We'd like to feel fearless about taking on new challenges. We want to feel powerful as we make new changes in our life and career. We're constantly having a dialogue with ourselves of what's okay and what's not okay. Our suffering comes from our stories, our perceptions about what we interpret about what's happening.

Confidence is something you give to yourself. In these 21 ways you've been introduced to some ways to build your self-confidence. Building confidence is learning more about yourself and making a choice of what positive changes need to happen.

This book is a collection of my personal development journey and experiences that helped me build my self-confidence. My hope is that you find some valuable ideas that will help you increase your confidence.

Final Thoughts

ncreasing confidence is an inner choice you make. Making a choice for your well-being and fulfillment is key in leading a happy and sustaining life.

As I shared about my life in this book you've noticed that many times, I was at choice in creating a change, a better circumstance for my personal development. For me, having self-confidence was important because this meant I would ignite my courage to try new environments and new people. This meant freedom to me.

Realize you are at choice every day of your life. Confidence is a choice. Freedom is a choice. Choosing to create a better version of yourself each day is a choice. Once you choose it you need to follow up with the actions that will give you the results you desire.

All success is comprised of two components: a choice/thought and a plan/action. Add confidence to the recipe and you have a recipe for living the life you desire.

I grew up in the baby boomer generation in which women were treated differently in the workplace and education. I witness men being groomed for promotion and advancement more than I saw women being taken seriously about advancements in the workplace.

I was a teenager when the Civil Rights Act of 1964 was passed by Congress. This act prohibits discrimination on the basis of race, color, religion, sex or national origin. From that time laws have been created that address discrimination for women in this country.

In writing this book, my goal is to support women who want advancement in their lives and career. In sharing my experiences, insights and education I hope to inspire other women to believe in themselves and build their confidence so they can go after creating a life of their dreams.

My coaching business and this book are for the woman who feels stuck and at the same time knows something is missing in her life. Throughout this book I describe different ways women can take action in increasing self-confidence and not surrender to fear.

You can contact me at https://www.inharmonycoaching. com/contact for more information about my coaching programs.

Acknowledgments

I want to give acknowledgement to all the mentors, teachers, coaches and friends who have helped me in reaching a level of confidence with my career and personal development.

I want to acknowledge Andrea Glass, who provided expert support with editing, proofreading and formatting for Kindle.

Karen Floyd is an amazing photographer and graphic artist and I appreciate her cover design for this book.

I want to acknowledge Michelle Wallace who helped with proofreading the first ten chapters.

I want to acknowledge Trisha Fuentes, who provided support in designing the interior book format for this book.

Eric Lofholm, my sales coach introduced me to writing a book in a day and how creating this book was a possibility that was reachable.

My deepest thanks go to all my wonderful colleagues, clients and friends who believed in me and supported me in completing this book.

About the Author

Laura Diaz is a board-certified life coach who has helped hundreds of clients increase their self-confidence and skills for success.

In 2011 she opened her coaching business, In Harmony Coaching. Since that time, she has been coaching clients in increasing their self-confidence and taking the next action in creating successful results in their careers and life.

She believes in continuing education and has engaged in several coaching programs after she completed her formal training as a life coach with Accomplishment Coaching Training Programs.

Choose Confidence: 21 Ways Women Can Increase Self-Confidence is a collection of personal experiences, personal development and principles that have helped Laura and others build confidence.

With Laura's experiences, learnings and challenges this valuable guide will benefit anyone who wants to move through life with confidence, ease and courage.

You can contact Laura at www.inharmonycoaching.com/contact to find out more about her coaching programs.

What's Next?

Dear readers,

The subject of confidence has no ending.

If you want to continue creating more insight into your confidence, we have coaching programs that you may find interesting. Every year, we develop new coaching group programs that will help you increase your confidence. You can find out more at https://www.inharmonycoaching.com.

Thank you for taking the time to read this book. I have enjoyed sharing my work with you.

I send out short articles in a newsletter to my subscribers. Subscribers are the first to hear about my newest coaching groups, webinars and coaching programs. We also provide several free webinars and free handouts throughout the year.

You can sign up for this free newsletter at:

https://www.inharmonycoaching.com/contact.

Made in the USA
Monee, IL
02 July 2021